Finish **STRONG**

To

....

From

....

More Than a Statement...
It's an Attitude

DAN GREEN

Finish **STRONG**

THOMAS NELSON
Since 1798

NASHVILLE   DALLAS   MEXICO CITY   RIO DE JANEIRO

Published in Nashville, Tennessee, by Thomas Nelson. Thomas Nelson is a registered trademark of Thomas Nelson, Inc.

Originally published by Simple Truths LLC

1952 McDowell Road, Suite 300

Naperville, IL 60563

Toll Free: 800.900.3427

www.simpletruths.com

This edition published under license from Simple Truths exclusively for Thomas Nelson Inc.

Thomas Nelson, Inc., titles may be purchased in bulk for educational, business, fund-raising, or sales promotional use. For information, please e-mail SpecialMarkets@ThomasNelson.com.

Unless otherwise noted, Scripture quotations are taken from THE NEW KING JAMES VERSION. © 1982 by Thomas Nelson, Inc. Used by permission. All rights reserved.

Scripture quotations marked NASB are from NEW AMERICAN STANDARD BIBLE®, © The Lockman Foundation 1960, 1962, 1963, 1968, 1971, 1972, 1973, 1975, 1977, 1995. Used by permission.

Scripture quotations marked MSG are from *The Message* by Eugene H. Peterson. © 1993, 1994, 1995, 1996, 2000. Used by permission of NavPress Publishing Group. All rights reserved.

Scripture quotations marked NIV are from the Holy Bible, New International Version®, NIV®. Copyright © 1973, 1978, 1984 by Biblica, Inc.™ Used by permission of Zondervan. All rights reserved worldwide. www.zondervan.com

ISBN: 978-1-4003-2087-5

Printed in China

12 13 14 15 16 RRD 6 5 4 3 2 1

www.thomasnelson.com

DEDICATION

To my parents for their infinite belief . . .

To my girls for their constant inspiration . . .

To my wife for her enduring love . . .

Finish STRONG

TABLE OF CONTENTS

INTRODUCTION

Finish strong.

I challenge you to find two words that more absolutely define a performance objective. For me, those two words are a clear call to action. The phrase *finish strong* perfectly conveys how the whole is greater than the sum of the parts.

When you combine finish *with* strong, *you create a powerful platform for action.*

It's not uncommon for these words to flow from the mouths of athletes in pre- and post-event interviews. The media uses this phrase to describe the performance of everything from the stock market to stock car racing. And for as long as we have documented history, the spirit of these words has existed. Consider, for instance, Jesus' story about workers who were blessed to receive their master's "Well done, good servant" (Luke 19:17). That commendation is a worthwhile goal not only for our lives but also for each one of our responsibilities along the way. We want not only to finish the race strong, but to finish every lap along the way strong as well.

BELIEVE
AND ACT AS IF
IT WERE
IMPOSSIBLE
TO FAIL.

CHARLES F. KETTERING

Regardless of what came before or of what is yet to come, what matters most right now is how I choose to respond to the challenge before me. Will I lie down or will I fight? The choice is mine, and I choose to

FINISH STRONG.

DAN GREEN

The phrase *finish strong* has become a driving force in my life. For more than ten years, it has been my personal mantra for achieving excellence in life, sports, and business. I have personally embraced the finish strong mindset in all aspects of my life. And when facing challenge or adversity, I remind myself first of God's presence with me and His power that is available to me and then of this truth:

Regardless of what came before or of what is yet to come, what matters most right now is how I choose to respond to the challenge before me. Will I lie down or will I fight? The choice is mine, and I choose to finish strong.

I don't always get the result I want. But in the times when I have had to trust in God's perfect plan for me and lean on my commitment, I have always felt a greater sense of accomplishment and satisfaction knowing that I gave it all I had.

The purpose of this book is to introduce you to the finish strong attitude and hope that you will embrace it, that you will make it your own personal goal to finish strong and that you will—and I'm describing this effort in different terms—do all things as unto the Lord (Colossians 3:17). You will read about some amazing people who exemplify the finish strong spirit in sports, business, and life. All of them illustrate lessons for life; a few point to the Giver of Life as the reason they finish strong. And my hope is that you, too, will always—by God's grace—finish strong.

DAN GREEN

Finish **STRONG**

Courage

Most of us have far more courage than
we ever dreamed we possessed.

DALE CARNEGIE

Be strong and of good courage;
do not be afraid, nor be dismayed,
for the Lord your God is with you
wherever you go.

JOSHUA 1:9

Courage is almost a contradiction in terms.
It means a strong desire to live taking
the form of a readiness to die.

GILBERT K. CHESTERTON

Finish **STRONG**

What's in a
NAME?

John Baker was too short and slight to be a runner for his high school track team. But John loved to run, and he wanted to make the team. His best friend, John Haaland, was a tall and promising runner who had been heavily recruited by the Manzano High School track coach, but he wanted nothing to do with the sport. John Baker asked the track coach to let him join the team under the condition that his best friend would follow. The coach agreed, and John Baker became a runner.

The team's first meet was a 1.7-mile cross-country race through the foothills of Albuquerque. Reigning state champion Lloyd Goff was running, and all eyes were on him. The race began, and the pack of runners led by Goff disappeared behind the hill. The spectators waited. A minute passed . . . then two . . . and three. Then the silhouette of a single runner appeared. The crowd assumed that it was one of the favorites. But to everyone's amazement, it was John Baker leading the way to the finish line. In his first meet, he blew away the field and set a new meet record.

When asked what happened behind the hill, John explained that at the halfway point of the run, he was struggling hard. He asked himself a question: ***Am I doing my best?***

Still unsure if he truly was giving his best effort, John fixed his eyes on the back of the runner in front of him.

One at a time, *he thought.*
He focused on just one thing—passing the runner in front of him.

He would let nothing distract him. Not fatigue, not pain, nothing. And, one by one, he caught and passed each runner until there was no one else to pass.

As the season progressed, John proved that his first race was not a fluke. Once the race began, the fun-loving, unassuming teenager became a fierce and relentless competitor who refused to lose. By the end of his junior year, John had broken six meet records and was largely regarded to be the best miler in the state. In his senior year, he ran the entire track and cross-country season undefeated and then won the state championship in both sports. The future certainly looked bright for the seventeen-year-old.

John entered the University of New Mexico in 1962, and he took his training to the next level by running more than ten miles a day. In the spring of 1965, his team faced the most feared team in track—the University of Southern California Trojans. There was little doubt that the mile belonged to the Trojans. During the race, John led for the first lap, then slipped back to fourth. At the far turn of the third lap, he collided with another runner vying

for position. Stumbling and struggling to stay on his feet, John lost valuable time. With just under 330 yards to go, he dug deep and, living up to his reputation, blew past the leaders to win the race by three seconds.

John Baker's future as a runner looked bright. After graduating from college, he set his sights on the 1972 Olympics. In order to have time to train and also make a living, John took a coaching position at Aspen Elementary in Albuquerque, where he had the opportunity to work with kids—something he had always wanted to do. Within a few months, Coach Baker became known as the coach who cared. He invested a great deal of time and energy into his students. Not at all a critical coach, he demanded of his athletes only what he demanded of himself: each runner's best effort. The kids responded and loved learning from Coach Baker.

> *Oh, the depth of the riches both of the wisdom and knowledge of God! How unsearchable are His judgments and unfathomable His ways!*
>
> { ROMANS 11:33 NASB }

In May 1969, just before his twenty-fifth birthday, John noticed that he was tiring prematurely during his workouts. Two weeks later he developed chest pains, and one morning he woke with a painfully swollen groin. He went to see his doctor, and they discovered that John had an advanced form of testicular cancer. The only chance John had was to undergo surgery. The operation confirmed the worst: John's cancer had spread. His doctor believed that he had, at best, six months to live—and even so, a second operation would be necessary.

What devastating news. How easy it would have been for John to feel sorry for himself and simply quit life. In fact, shortly before the second operation, John drove to the mountains prepared to do exactly that. He did not want to put his family through the pain. Just before he drove off the cliff, though, he recalled the faces of his children at Aspen and wondered if they would think that this was the best Coach Baker could do. Suicide was not the legacy he wanted to leave behind. At that moment John decided to rededicate his life to those kids. He was not a quitter. He drove home determined to give his best effort each of the days he had left.

In September, after extensive surgery and a summer of treatments, John returned to Aspen and started a unique program that involved handicapped kids in the sports program. He appointed kids as Coach's Timekeeper or

Chief Equipment Supervisor, and everyone who wanted to participate was included. By Thanksgiving, letters from parents in praise of Coach Baker were arriving daily at Aspen Elementary. John also created a special award for any child he thought deserved recognition. He used his own trophies as awards—after carefully polishing off his own name. He purchased special fabric with his own money, and at night he would cut out blue ribbons to give as awards.

> ### *"If anyone desires to be first, he shall be . . . servant of all."*
>
> { MARK 9:35 }

John refused to take medication to help with his pain because he was afraid it would impair his ability to work with his kids. In early 1970, John was asked to help coach a small Albuquerque track club for girls—the Duke City Dashers. By that summer the Dashers were a team to contend with. Baker boldly predicted that they would make it to the Amateur Athletic Union finals.

By now, Baker's condition was complicated by the chemotherapy treatments. He could not keep any food down, his health rapidly deteriorated, and he struggled to make it to practices. But at one October practice, a girl ran up to Coach Baker and shouted, "Coach, your prediction came true!

We're going to the AAU championship next month!" Baker was elated—and hoped he would live long enough to go along. Unfortunately, that was not to be. A few weeks later, John collapsed. He would not be able to make the trip. On Thanksgiving Day in 1970, at the age of twenty-six—and eighteen months after his first visit to the doctor—John Baker passed away. He had beaten the odds by twelve months. Two days later, the Duke City Dashers won the AAU championship in St. Louis . . . in honor of Coach Baker.

A few days after his funeral, the children at Aspen Elementary began calling their school "John Baker School." When others rapidly adopted this change, a movement began to make the new name official. The Aspen principal referred the matter to the Albuquerque school board, and in the spring of 1971, 520 families voted on the matter. There were 520 votes for the name change, none against. That May, at a ceremony attended by hundreds of the beloved coach's family members, friends, and kids, Aspen Elementary officially became John Baker Elementary.

Today, John Baker Elementary stands as a monument to a courageous young man who believed in giving his best effort right down to the very end of his days. The John Baker Foundation carries on his legacy. The following poem—written by John five years before he was diagnosed with cancer—is used with the permission of that foundation.

Many thoughts race through my mind
As I step up to the starting line

Butterflies through my stomach fly,
And as I free that last deep sigh,

I feel that death is drawing near,
But the end of the race I do not fear.

For when the string comes across my breast,
I know it's time for eternal rest.

The gun goes off, the race is run,
And only God knows if I've won.

My family and friends and many more
Can't understand what it was for.

But this "Race to Death" is a final test,
And I'm not afraid, for I've done my best.

JOHN BAKER

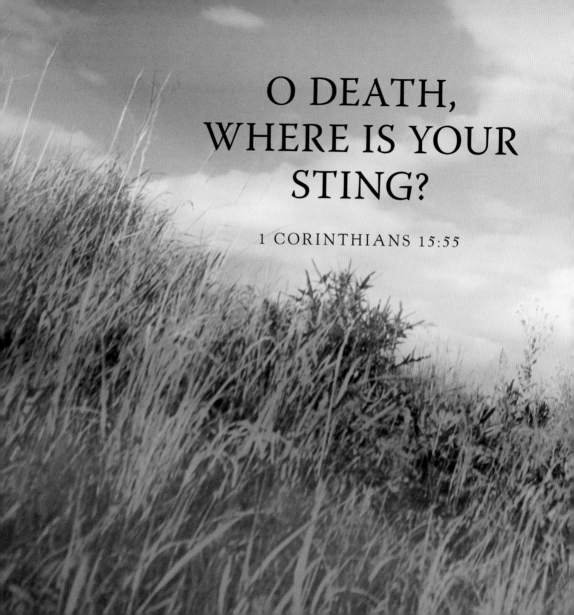

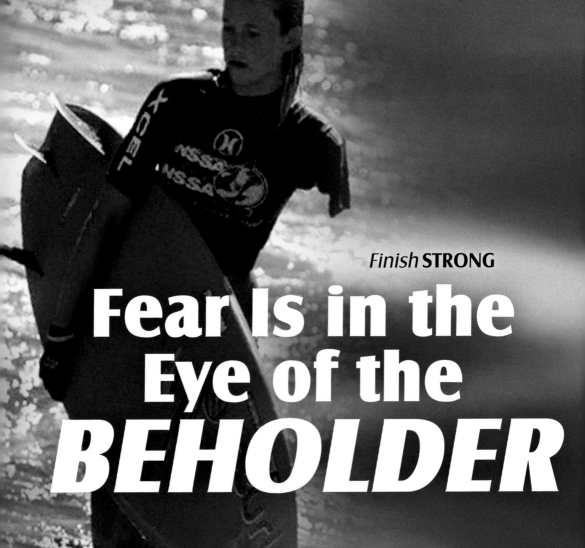

Finish **STRONG**

Fear Is in the Eye of the *BEHOLDER*

It was a perfect day for surfing off the coast of Kauai. The thirteen-year-old surfing protégé had just finished riding a twenty-foot wave and was lying facedown on her surfboard. As she paddled out to catch another wave, her hope of becoming a professional surfer appeared to be destroyed in an instant. Without warning, she felt a tug on her left arm, and in a split second she realized that she'd been attacked by a shark.

As she struggled to gain her composure, she realized something even more horrifying: the fourteen-foot tiger shark had bitten clean through her board, taking her left arm with it in a single bite. Suddenly, survival took priority over surfing.

Bethany Hamilton had learned to surf at the age of four. When she was eight, she entered her first contest and won both of the events she competed in. At the age of ten, she placed first in the Under-11 girls division, first in the U-15 girls, and second in the U-12 boys division at the Volcom Pufferfish Surf Series. She was determined to become a professional surfer, and she was definitely on track to make that happen. Then, in a single violent moment on that fall day in 2003, it seemed her dream was shattered.

Bethany, however, was born with the heart of a lion and the competitive spirit of a thorough-bred. She was determined to return to surfing. Depending on her family, her friends, and her faith in God, Bethany recovered rapidly. Within ten weeks of the attack, she was surfing again. Convinced she could overcome her physical challenge, she worked hard to learn to surf around her disability. But she also had to over-come the psychological fear of another attack. Bethany would face her fears by singing and praying when she was out on the water.

FEAR NOT,
FOR I AM WITH YOU;
BE NOT DISMAYED,
FOR I AM YOUR GOD.
I WILL STRENGTHEN YOU,
YES, I WILL HELP YOU,
I WILL UPHOLD YOU WITH
MY RIGHTEOUS RIGHT HAND.

ISAIAH 41:10

Then, incredibly, less than a year after her attack, Bethany returned to competition and took fifth place at the National Surfing Championships and first place at the first event for the Hawaii National Scholastic Surfing Association. In 2004, ESPN honored her with an ESPY Award as Best Comeback Athlete of the Year.

Bethany's ability to overcome her physical and mental challenges puts her in an elite class. She chose to *finish strong*.

Her choice to confront her fears and continue working toward her goals is a powerful picture of courage.

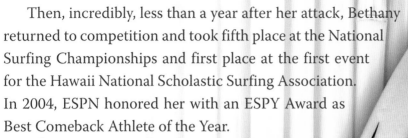

I can do all things through Christ who strengthens me.

PHILIPPIANS 4:13

COURAGE doesn't mean you don't get afraid. Courage means you don't let fear stop you.

Bethany Hamilton

Finish **STRONG**

Faith

All things work together for good to those who love God, to those who are the called according to His purpose.

ROMANS 8:28

The only thing that stands between a person and what they want in life is the will to try it and the faith to believe it possible.

RICH DEVOS

"All things are possible to him who believes."

MARK 9:23

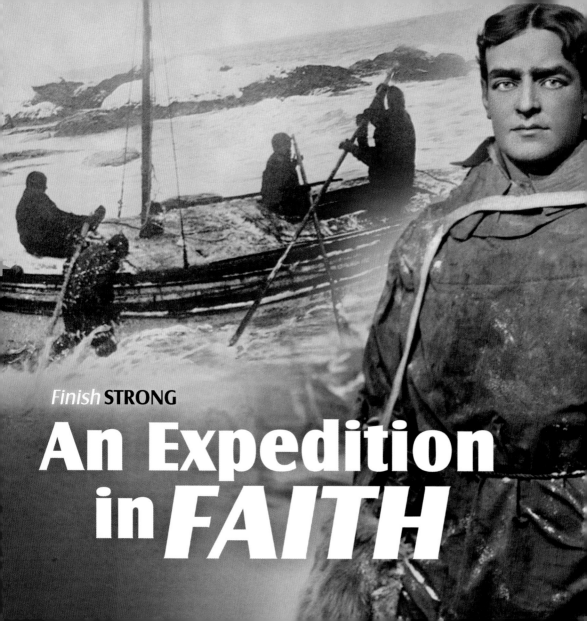

Finish **STRONG**

An Expedition
in *FAITH*

On August 1, 1914, Sir Ernest Shackleton set sail with a crew of twenty-eight on an expedition to the Antarctic. Their goal was to cross the Antarctic on foot, something that had never been done. Shackleton was already a successful and highly respected explorer known for his determination, conviction, and faith in God, the Creator of the world. Shackleton loved to explore. He had been knighted for his successful 1907–1909 expedition to Antarctica. No wonder Shackleton received five thousand applications for the twenty-eight available positions. Many people believe that he placed the following ad in a London newspaper to attract applicants:

MEN WANTED

For hazardous journey. Small wages, bitter cold, long months of complete darkness, constant danger, safe return doubtful. Honour and recognition in case of success.

While there is no evidence that this ad actually ran, it nevertheless aptly describes the task that Shackleton was trying to recruit for.

Five months into the expedition, their ship, *Endurance*, became stuck in the heavy ice floes near Antarctica, which is not a rare occurrence. Believing that the ice would eventually recede and the ship would be freed, Shackleton kept focused on the expedition. However, over the following three weeks, the ship became solidly frozen in the ice; attempts to free her were futile. At the end of February in 1915, the crew prepared the ship to become their camp for the remainder of the winter.

I AM PERSUADED THAT NEITHER DEATH NOR LIFE, NOR ANGELS NOR PRINCIPALITIES NOR POWERS, NOR THINGS PRESENT NOR THINGS TO COME, NOR HEIGHT NOR DEPTH, NOR ANY OTHER CREATED THING, SHALL BE ABLE TO SEPARATE US FROM THE LOVE OF GOD WHICH IS IN CHRIST JESUS OUR LORD.

ROMANS 8:38-39

At this point, Shackleton abandoned his initial goal. Now he was focused on returning to England with his entire crew.

In October, eight months after *Endurance* first got stuck, the pressure caused by the ice started breaking the ship apart, making it uninhabitable. When the order to abandon ship was given, the entire crew tried to salvage as many supplies as they could. Taking the sled dogs, food, gear, and three lifeboats, they moved their camp to the ice floe next to their sinking ship. The temperatures were brutal, reaching -15°F on average. For the next five months, the expedition camped on the ice floe, surviving on what little food they had left.

A man's heart plans his way, but the LORD directs his steps.
{ PROVERBS 16:9 }

In April, the ice floe they were camped on began to break apart. Shackleton ordered the crew to take only essential supplies and board the lifeboats. They fled the disintegrating ice floe and traveled seven days by sea to Elephant Island, a barren place made up mostly of rock-covered snow with temperatures reaching -20°F. For the next nine months, under Shackleton's leadership, the broken expedition remained loyal, optimistic, focused, and faithful to their leader's belief that they would survive—and their leader remained steadfast in his faith in his God.

Shackleton's plan for his crew's survival depended on his ability to reach a whaling outpost that was more than eight hundred miles across the most treacherous seas in the world. Determined to save his crew, Shackleton set out with five crew members in one of the lifeboats. The odds of making it were one in a hundred, but Shackleton successfully made it to the outpost and four months later returned to Elephant Island with a rescue party. Nautical scholars consider this journey by lifeboat to be one of the greatest accomplishments in maritime history.

On August 30, 1916—after twenty-two months of being stranded on a barren rock in subzero temperatures—the crew of Endurance *was rescued. All twenty-eight crew members survived the ordeal, and most were quick to credit their leader's strong faith as key to their survival.*

The eye of
the Lᴏʀᴅ is on
those who fear
Him, on those
who hope in
His *MERCY*.

Psalm 33:18

GREAT IS YOUR
FAITHFULNESS.

LAMENTATIONS 3:23

Finish STRONG

It Ain't Over TILL IT'S OVER

As the 2004 Summer Olympics in Athens neared, expectations were very high for Paul Hamm, the reigning world champion and the first US man to ever win a world all-around title. No American had ever won the men's all-around Olympic gold medal in gymnastics, and Paul was expected to change that. (The only US gymnast to ever medal was Peter Vidmar in the 1984 Olympics.)

Paul started out strong: after the first three events, he was in first place in the all-around by .038 points. Then disaster struck. During his vault performance, he under-rotated and missed his landing, causing him to sit down and nearly fall off the platform.

This cardinal sin of gymnastics significantly impacted his score. After the vault competition was over, Paul found himself in twelfth place. I remember watching the telecast and seeing him sitting on the sidelines with a pale look on his face. At that point in time, he clearly believed he had blown his chance to make gymnastics history.

We also glory in tribulations, knowing that tribulation produces perseverance; and perseverance, character; and character, hope.

ROMANS 5:3–4

But then Paul Hamm demonstrated the difference between mediocrity and greatness. He chose to put his fall behind him and move forward. He gave his best effort in order to finish strong. First up at his next event, he pulled off a great routine on the parallel bars and nailed his dismount. This solid performance plus the struggles of some of his competitors helped Paul move into fourth place in the all-around, and his last and strongest event—the high bar—was still to come.

Paul was determined to take advantage of this positive turn of events and make sure that he won at least the bronze medal. After all, he was a master of the high bar, and he had scripted a highly technical routine in order to have a shot at earning the most points possible. And Paul would be the last competitor to go.

As I watched the broadcast, I could see Paul pour his heart into his routine. I could feel his energy, focus, and determination. When he nailed his dismount, it was electrifying, and even before his score was revealed, Paul's face showed that in his own mind he had won, regardless of the outcome. He had won by coming back after a crushing failure on the vault and proving to himself that he could perform—and perform brilliantly— after failure. And that spectacular performance marked one of the most dramatic comebacks in all of sports. Paul Hamm won the gold medal in the men's all-around by 0.012 points, becoming the first US man to ever win the Olympic title. Talk about finishing strong!

Finish **STRONG**

Belief

The will to do springs from the
knowledge that we can do.

JAMES ALLEN

To accomplish great things,
we must not only act, but also dream;
not only plan, but also believe.

ANATOLE FRANCE

"Blessed are those who have not seen
and yet have believed."

JOHN 20:29

Finish **STRONG**

A Spirit Forged in *STEEL*

On June 23, 1940, Wilma Glodean Rudolph was born prematurely, weighing only four and a half pounds. Wilma was the twentieth of Ed and Blanche Rudolph's twenty-two children. The Rudolphs were African Americans living in a time of segregation. Since the local hospital was for whites only and since the Rudolphs had little money, Mrs. Rudolph was forced to care for Wilma herself. The early years were very rough. Wilma's mother nursed her through one illness after another—measles, mumps, scarlet fever, chicken pox, and double pneumonia.

A few years after Wilma's birth, her parents discovered that her left leg and foot were not developing normally and, consequently, were becoming deformed. Doctors told Blanche that Wilma had polio, that she would never walk, and that she would have to wear steel braces on her legs. Refusing to accept this diagnosis, Mrs. Rudolph set out to find a cure. She discovered that Wilma could receive treatment at Meharry Hospital in Nashville.

The Rudolphs also relied on their faith in God, the Great Physician. When young Wilma would ask if she would ever walk, her parents pointed her to her good God: "Honey, you only have to believe. You have to trust in God because with God all things are possible."

For the next two years, Mrs. Rudolph drove Wilma fifty miles each way to physical therapy appointments. Eventually, the hospital staff taught Mrs. Rudolph how to do the exercises at home. Everyone in the family worked with Wilma, providing her with encouragement to be strong and to get better. Thanks to the patience, support, effort, and love she received from her family, at the age of twelve, Wilma could walk normally without the assistance of crutches, braces, or corrective shoes. Having spent a great deal of her life limited by her illnesses, Wilma felt a freedom she had never felt before. It was then that Wilma decided to become an athlete.

"With God nothing will be impossible."
(LUKE 1:37)

Wilma chose to pursue basketball first, just as her older sister had. For three years she rode the bench, not playing in a single game. But Wilma's spirit had been forged from steel, and she continued to practice hard, refusing to give up. In her sophomore year she became the starting guard for the team and subsequently led the team to a state championship. But Wilma's first love was running. At the age of sixteen (barely four years free of braces), Wilma participated in track at the 1956 Olympics and won a bronze medal in the 4 x 100–meter relay. However, it was at the state basketball tournament that she was first spotted by Ed Temple, the coach for the women's track team at Tennessee State University. Ed recruited Wilma on a track scholarship and changed the course of her athletic pursuits.

Wilma's most famous athletic accomplishment happened during the 1960 Rome Olympics. The little girl who could hardly walk without the assistance of crutches or braces had completely overcome her physical limitations, and she became the first American woman to win three gold medals in a single Olympics.

My mother taught me
very early to believe
I could achieve any
accomplishment
I wanted to.
The first was to walk
without braces.

Wilma Rudolph

YEAR	AGE	EVENT	MEDAL	RESULT
1956	16	4X100M RELAY WOMEN	BRONZE	44.9
1960	20	100M WOMEN	GOLD	11.0
1960	20	200M WOMEN	GOLD	24.0
1960	20	4X100M RELAY WOMEN	GOLD	44.5

Finish **STRONG**
Follow the
SUN

Ben Hogan was nine years old when his father committed suicide right in front of him, and this horrifying experience had a deep impact on that little boy. Ben eventually turned to golf as a way to escape the horrors of his childhood. He was a caddie at a local course in Ft. Worth, Texas, where he would hit balls after work until dark. Golf was the perfect game for Ben because it did not require him to interact with anyone. And he loved the game, especially the way it felt when he executed a perfect golf shot. Some days he hit so many golf balls that his hands would bleed.

At the age of seventeen, Ben set his sights on perfecting the game he loved so much and set out on the professional tour. Failing to make it on the tour, he was forced to take a full-time job.

Yet he continued to practice his golf. He believed that he had what it took to be a great golfer.

A few years later, Ben once again attempted to make the tour. In the process he met his wife-to-be, Valerie. An instant inspiration to Ben, she traveled with him from tournament to tournament—and back then the professional golf tour schedule was established based on where in the country the sun stayed out the longest. The golfers would follow the sun as they traveled from one week to the next.

During these early years, Ben struggled to make a living. On one other occasion, he was forced to give up the game for a job with a steady income. But he continued to practice his golf game and, with the encouragement of his wife, returned to the tour for a third try. Then in 1940, eleven years after turning pro, Ben Hogan won his first professional tournament. For the next four years, Ben had modest success on the PGA tour, but on and off the course he had an intense focus and concentration that suggested a cold and unfriendly personality. Often, for instance, Ben walked from shot to shot with his head down, staring at his shoelaces. When he did look up, Ben's steely grey stare would instantly intimidate anyone who caught his glance.

Ultimately, this look earned him both the nickname "The Hawk" and the reputation for being an ice-cold and fierce competitor.

In 1944, just as Ben was beginning to experience success on the tour, he decided to serve his country by joining the US Air Force. During his military service, Ben's time for playing golf was limited. He would read news articles about the great success of his fellow competitor Byron Nelson, who was dominating the PGA tour. Nelson's record of eleven wins in one year still stands today, and it will probably never be broken. At the time, the press anointed Nelson "Mr. Golf" and "Lord Byron." Both frustrated and motivated by Byron's success and notoriety, Ben Hogan returned to golf in 1945 determined to establish himself as the strongest player in the game. And he did. For the next three years, Ben dominated the sport by winning.

31 EVENTS,
2 PGA CHAMPIONSHIPS,
AND THE *US OPEN.*

In 1949, Ben and Valerie were taking a break from the tour. Driving back to Texas, they ran into a dense fog that forced Ben to slow down to less than ten miles per hour. In a split second, a bus pulled out to pass a truck and was in the direct path of the Hogans' car. In a selfless act, Ben threw himself in front of Valerie to protect her from the impact. The bus hit them head-on, sending the engine into the driver's seat and the steering column into the backseat. Ben would have been killed instantly if he had not tried to protect his wife. Because of his unselfish courage, Valerie suffered only minor injuries, but the crash left Ben clinging to life.

Ben fractured his pelvis, collarbone, and left ankle, and blood clots threatened his life—forcing the doctors to limit his blood circulation by tying off principal veins in his legs. The doctors said it was unlikely he would ever walk again, let alone play professional golf. But Ben was a fierce and determined competitor, not only in sport but also in life. Determined to over-come the challenges confronting him and supported by his wife, Ben recovered. He persevered and gained enough strength to return to golf in 1950, just eleven months after the accident.

In his first tournament back, Ben forced a play-off with Sam Snead, which was quite an amazing accomplishment. However, Ben's physical condition caused him to fade in the play-off and ultimately lose to Snead. Even so, this success proved to Ben that he could compete. He continued to practice hard, and today Ben Hogan is credited with being the first professional golfer to actually practice. When asked about this, he replied, "You hear stories about me beating my brains out practicing, but . . . I was enjoying myself. I couldn't wait to get up in the morning so I could hit balls. When I'm hitting the ball where I want, hard and crisply, it's a joy that very few people experience." Five months later, he would win the US Open, reinforcing his belief in himself.

After the accident, however, Ben's legs were never the same. He could hardly walk eighteen holes, so he limited himself to seven tournaments each year. Yet for the next three years, Ben Hogan dominated every tournament he entered, winning thirteen of the tournaments he entered, six of which were majors. In 1953, Ben Hogan entered only six tournaments, but he won five of them, including three majors. And winning three majors in a single year was a record that stood for almost fifty years until 2000, when Tiger Woods accomplished the same feat.

"Greater love
has no one than
this, than to lay
down one's life
for his friends."

John 15:13

64 VICTORIES

Ben Hogan would ultimately retire with sixty-four professional victories and nine major titles—six of which came after the car crash. He is known today as the father of the modern golf swing, and Tiger Woods and Jack Nicklaus consider him to be the best ball striker the game has ever seen.

One of his greatest contributions to the game, however, is the concept of practicing. Before Ben Hogan, the idea of practicing the game of golf did not exist. His work ethic and commitment to improvement is now the model for today's touring professionals.

Ben Hogan overcame a dark childhood memory, early failure at the game of golf, and a debilitating car crash to truly become one of the legends of golf. He continued to be an ambassador of the game and charitable organizations long after his retirement. At different points throughout his life, Ben Hogan could have simply been finished. Instead he chose to persevere, to fight, and ultimately to finish strong.

Finish STRONG

BELIEVE
in Miracles

It was 1980, and the US economy was in a recession. Iran had taken Americans hostage, and the Russians had invaded Afghanistan. With the Cold War in full force, President Carter threatened to boycott the Moscow Summer Olympics as a way of protesting Russia's actions in Afghanistan. Across America, the events of the time were driving American pride and morale to an all-time low. But a hockey game was about to change all of that . . .

In the 1980 Winter Olympics at Lake Placid, the USA hockey team was comprised of college kids, some with pro hockey aspirations. Under the guidance of Coach Herb Brooks, these young American athletes became a fast, well-conditioned, and cohesive team. While some viewed Brooks's coaching methods as somewhat questionable, they did result in the development of a physically and mentally tough young hockey team.

Brooks knew how dangerous his team could be. He also knew that many of their competitors were underestimating his team's potential and had written them off as a non-contender. Brooks planned to use this miscalculation to his team's advantage.

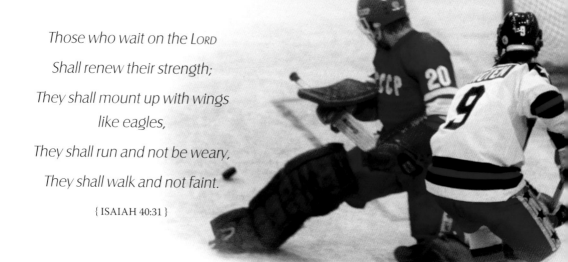

*Those who wait on the L*ORD

Shall renew their strength;

They shall mount up with wings
*   like eagles,*

They shall run and not be weary,

They shall walk and not faint.

{ ISAIAH 40:31 }

In order to make it to the medal round, the USA team had to fight hard in each match. In the opening game against Sweden, they scored with twenty-seven seconds remaining to force a 2–2 tie. This was a significant event because the Americans had not beaten the Swedes since 1960. The tie lifted the team's morale and planted that first seed of belief. Next, the Americans dominated a strong Czech team by winning 7–3, with seven different Americans scoring. Again, this was another significant event for the young team because the Czechs had been widely expected to have a lock on the silver medal. The USA team would continue its way through the bracket by winning its next three games, ultimately positioning themselves for the first medal round against the Russians. Belief had turned into passion for the Americans.

The young USA team had been given essentially no chance at beating the stronger Russian team. The Russians had dominated Olympic hockey for years, and their players were considered professionals by all accounts because of the European hockey league's strength and the financial backing of the Soviet Union. The Soviets took great pride in their dominance. In fact, just before the start of the Olympics, they crushed the young American team 10–3 in an exhibition match at Madison Square Garden. It was a humiliating loss in front of American fans, and the Russians clearly seemed destined for gold.

Fast-forward a few weeks, and the USA team found itself up against the Soviets in the first medal round, battling not only for a medal, but also for the pride of America. With tension between Russia and the United States very high, this hockey game took on greater meaning for both nations.

The Russians started strong and took a 2–1 lead early in the first period. With the final seconds winding down in the first period, the Russians made a critical mistake. Thinking that the period was almost over, they backed off and began skating off the ice. There was, however, just enough time for USA's Mark Johnson to take a rebounded shot with one second left and drill it into the Russians' net. The USA had tied the game 2–2. The Russians would score quickly again in the second period, and again the Americans would answer, resulting in a 3–3 tie going into the third period. The Russians had thrown everything they had at the Americans, and the young team had answered each blow with a goal of its own. Now, the Americans no longer believed that they could beat the Russians; they *knew* they could.

Midway through the third period, Mike Euruzione, the team captain, caught the puck and fired it past the Russian goaltender to give the Americans a 4–3 lead with ten minutes remaining. The field house erupted! Could the American team actually pull this off? Ten minutes seemed like an eternity. Team USA would need to finish strong if they were to hold off the Russian assault. And the Russians fought hard, firing ten shots for every one shot the USA team attempted. The level of emotion and energy in the rink was unimaginable. As the time wound down, the American fans began the chant "U-S-A, U-S-A." This passion was not about a hockey game. It was about American pride. The well-conditioned USA team held off the Russians and won. They finished strong in what became known as the Miracle on Ice.

Today, almost thirty years later, most people believe that this unlikely victory resulted in a gold medal for the USA. It did not. The win over the Russians put Team USA through to the next round, where they would defeat Finland to win the gold. In six of seven games played, the USA team came back from a deficit to win. They truly embodied the spirit of belief, persistence, and passion—and they definitely finished strong.

Truth can hold more surprises than fiction!

Do you believe in miracles?

AL MICHAELS, SPORTS BROADCASTER
AS TIME RAN OUT IN THE GAME

Finish STRONG
Attitude

Life is 10 percent what
you make it and 90
percent how you take it.

IRVING BERLIN

How you respond to the challenge
in the second half will determine
what you become after the game,
whether you are a winner or loser.

LOU HOLTZ

Whatever things are true, whatever things are
noble, whatever things are just, whatever things
are pure, whatever things are lovely,
whatever things are of good report, if
there is any virtue and if there is anything
praiseworthy—meditate on these things.

PHILIPPIANS 4:8

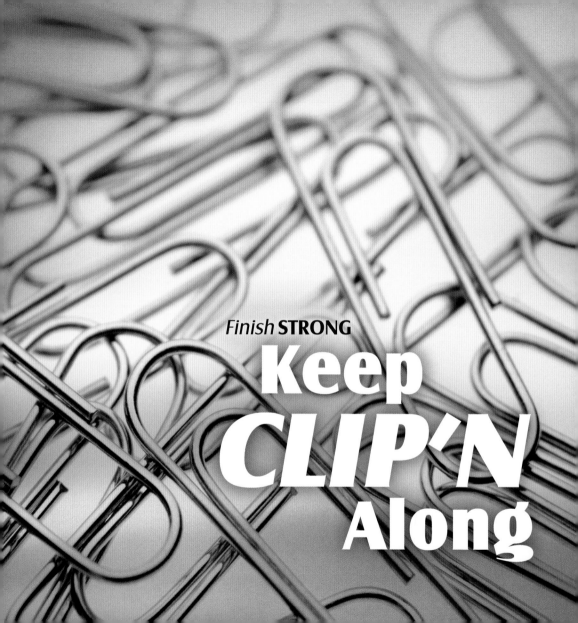

In the early nineties, when I was selling software systems to commercial banks, I discovered the power of the mind-set to finish strong. I spent a great deal of my time prospecting for leads over the phone. No matter how good you are at selling over the phone, it can be challenging to push yourself to make one more call—and a key to success in selling is making that one more call.

To help myself set a daily goal and meet it,
I started each day in the office by taking
twenty-five paper clips from the holder
and putting them on a coaster right next to the holder,
which was next to the phone.

Each time I engaged in a meaningful selling conversation, I would take one paper clip from the pile and put it back in the holder. I knew that having twenty-five significant selling conversations each day would enable me to reach my sales goals. So I made the commitment to myself not to leave the office until every paper clip was back in the holder. Many times the workday would be over for everyone else, but I had one paper clip sitting on that coaster. Finishing strong that day meant having one more selling conversation—and I dialed until I succeeded. I never left a paper clip sitting on the coaster, and I never put one back that I did not earn. The amount of activity generated by those phone calls filled my sales pipeline with opportunities.

*My career took off,
and I tripled my income
in the course of two years—
simply because I chose
to finish strong.*

The most important thing about goals is *HAVING ONE.*

Geoffrey Abert

Finish STRONG

To Finish
First You Must
FIRST
FINISH

Because of the success I achieved in sales, I had the good fortune to pursue another passion of mine—motorsports. I had a dream to race at the Indy 500. (I like to dream big.) Living in Indianapolis at the time, I was overexposed to the world of motorsports, and it was intoxicating. So I went to racing school to learn to drive open-wheel racecars. After I had spent a year racing in the Skip Barber Race Series, a racing friend of mine (who actually did try to qualify for Indy) took me under his wing. His brother owned a race team in Texas, and I signed up to race one of his Formula Fords in the Sports Car Club of America series (SCCA).

My first race was in October 1993 at Gateway International Raceway in St. Louis, Missouri. I was able to hang with the leaders for the first quarter of the race, but they were a bit quicker than I was. By the midpoint, they had pulled into a half-lap lead. I became a bit frustrated and began pushing the limits of my car in an effort to catch them. As a result, I pushed my car deep into a corner and lost control, spinning out and losing valuable time. Fortunately I was able to get back on track quickly, but it seemed unlikely that I could catch the leaders.

The LORD is my strength and song.
(PSALM 118:14)

I was devastated by my mistake.
Winning now seemed totally out of reach.

But I realized as I sped down the backstretch, with the cars behind me quickly catching up, that I had a decision to make. Would I get down on myself and coast around the final laps in despair? Or would I pull my belt tight, put my nose down, and set a realistic new goal? Having long been committed to finishing strong, I decided to try to turn the fastest lap of the race. I remember saying out loud, "Come on, Dan! Finish strong!"

Having taken control of my emotions, I got going. My vision cleared, everything around me slowed down, and my focus became intense. On the second to the last lap, I passed two cars. Coming out of the last turn with one lap to go, I could barely see the two leaders at the end of the front stretch diving into turn one. As I came through the first turn, I was shocked to see that the number one and two cars ahead of me had crashed and, as a result, taken themselves out of the race. I couldn't believe it! Coming out of the last turn, I saw the checkered flag waving. I had won! I was shocked. Had I given up after my spin, I never would have passed the two cars in front of me and put myself in a position to win. By choosing to finish strong, I won the first SCCA race I entered.

In racing they say that in order to finish first, you must first finish. True, but finishing strong is even better.

SUCCESS SEEMS TO BE
CONNECTED WITH
ACTION. SUCCESSFUL
PEOPLE KEEP
MOVING. THEY MAKE
MISTAKES, BUT THEY
DON'T QUIT.

CONRAD HILTON

Finish STRONG
Commitment

Don't be afraid to take a big step if one is indicated. You can't cross a chasm in two small jumps.

DAVID LLOYD GEORGE

Commit your way to the LORD; trust in him and he will do this.

PSALM 37:5 NIV

Keep on going, and the chances are that you will stumble on something, perhaps when you are least expecting it. I never heard of anyone ever stumbling on something sitting down.

CHARLES KETTERING

DYING
to Make a
Difference

After a two-year battle with cancer, teenager Miles Levin lost his fight. However, during his final years, he demonstrated a level of self-awareness, courage, and wisdom that most of us will never attain. Miles posted his thoughts on a carepages.com blog and, through this writing, encouraged thousands of people. He wrote with amazing grace and eloquence. Some of his posts were short:

"Dying is not what scares me.
It's dying having no impact."

Others were long and philosophical. But every post challenged the reader to think more deeply about living, dying, and making a difference.

Teach us to number our days,
that we may gain a heart of wisdom.
{ PSALM 90:12 }

Here's what Miles wrote just one month after being diagnosed with terminal cancer:

> I went to the driving range the other day, and I was thinking. . . .
> I was thinking how you start out with a big bucket full of golf balls,
> and you just start hitting away carelessly. Since you have dozens of
> them, each individual ball means nothing to you, so you just hit,
> hit, hit. One ball gone is practically inconsequential when sub-
> tracted from your bottomless bucket. There are no practice swings
> or technique reevaluations after a bad shot, because so many
> more tries remain.
>
> Yet, eventually, you start to have to reach down toward the
> bottom of the bucket to scavenge for another shot, and you realize
> that your tries are running out. With just a handful left, each swing
> becomes more meaningful, and the right technique becomes
> more crucial. So after each shot you take a couple practice swings
> and a few deep breaths.
>
> There is a very strong need to end on a good note. Even if
> every preceding shot was terrible, getting it right at the end means
> a lot. You know as you tee up your last ball, "This is my final shot,
> and I want to crush this with perfection. I must make this count!"
> Limited quantities and limited time bring a new, precious value
> and significance to anything you do. Live every day shooting as if
> it's your last shot. I know I have to.
>
> MILES ALPERN LEVIN, JULY 7, 2005

I have tried my best to show what it is to persevere and what it means to be strong.

Miles Levin

Just as Miles suggested, we should treat each day as precious, as one of a finite number of swings we take in life. So take your time, take a breath, and take a practice swing. Make every shot count and, most of all, finish strong!

Finish **STRONG**

Overnight
SUCCESS

Finishing strong in life, sports, or business does not always involve overcoming a challenge in a single moment. Sometimes it can take a lifetime to see the fruit of your efforts to finish strong. Such was the case for a man named William.

Read what historian and biographer Kevin Belmonte notes:

Harriet Beecher Stowe praised him in the pages of *Uncle Tom's Cabin*. Novelist E. M. Forester compared him to Gandhi. Abraham Lincoln invoked his memory in a celebrated speech. In the houses of Parliament, Nelson Mandela recalled his tireless labors on behalf of the sons and daughters of Africa, calling Britain "the land of William Wilberforce—who dared to stand up to demand that the slaves in our country should be freed."

In 1787, William Wilberforce became leader of the parliamentary campaign of the Committee for the Abolition of the Slave Trade. In May 1789, he made his first major speech on the subject. Two years later, in April of 1791, Wilberforce introduced a parliamentary bill to abolish the slave trade, a bill that was easily defeated 163 votes to 88. Six subsequent attempts to pass the bill also failed, the last time in 1805. Like any great leader, Wilberforce had cast his vision clearly, but he didn't easily reach his goal. Still, he persisted.

Here am I! Send me.

{ ISAIAH 6:8 }

Two years later, the bill came before Parliament again, and this time the results were different. In March 1807, the Slave Trade Act passed, abolishing the slave trade from the British Empire. It was a momentous victory, yet it was not Wilberforce's ultimate objective. He was working for the emancipation of all slaves. Finally, on July 26, 1833—over forty-five years after starting out—Wilberforce received news that this bill for the abolition of slavery had passed on its third reading in the House of Commons. Wilberforce died three days later, but the momentum he created saw his vision through to completion. One month after his death, Parliament passed the Slavery Abolition Act, giving freedom to every slave in the British Empire.

Have the dogged *DETERMINATION* to follow through to achieve your goal, regardless of circumstances or whatever other people say, think, or do.

Paul J. Meyer

Nothing changes until something moves.

ALBERT EINSTEIN

It doesn't matter where you've been;
it only matters where you are going.

BRIAN TRACY

The secret to success is
consistency of purpose.

BENJAMIN DISRAELI

Finish **STRONG**

REDEFINE
Your Limits

The ABC commentator called it one of the most defining moments in sports. After leading the 1982 Kona, Hawaii, triathlon for more than seven hours, Julie Moss collapsed fifty feet from the finish line. Millions of television viewers painfully watched Julie stagger . . . fall . . . stagger . . . fall . . . stagger . . . and finally crawl across the finish line. This was a defining moment in Julie's life.

Julie was a twenty-three-year-old student participating in her first triathlon, motivated in large part by her desire to do research for her exercise physiology thesis. She entered the event believing it would provide her with valuable experience she could draw on for her thesis. She did not consider herself an exceptional athlete. In fact, she says of her high school gym days, "I used to dread getting called onto the court for volleyball or having to serve in tennis."

"I really wasn't ready for the pressure of leading the race."

Leading an Ironman can have a powerful effect on people, and Julie experienced that firsthand. During the midpoint of the final leg—the marathon-distance 26.2-mile run—Julie's desire simply to finish began to evolve into the desire to finish first. Never in her life had she felt that competitive drive. She was, however, also about to experience the effects of her

50 YARDS

poor diet and insufficient hydration during the race. At that time, very little was known about how nutrition and hydration impact high-performance activity. The PowerBar hadn't been invented, and most athletes believed that bananas and water were the nutritional staples for high performance. We know otherwise today.

With about seven miles to go, Julie was forced to take breaks from her running and walk for a while. Her body was beginning to shut down. "It took all my focus just to keep my body working," she recalls. "I had to concentrate so much on how I placed my foot on the ground. If I was off by a bit, my leg would just buckle."

When she had just one hundred yards to go, Julie's mind began to play tricks on her. Imagining herself running across the finish line, she kept trying to run instead of walk to the finish. Later she said that she probably would have won the race if she had simply decided to walk instead of run. Instead, for the last fifty yards, she continued to fall, rise, step . . . fall, rise, step . . . fall,

TO FINISH

rise, step . . . over and over again. It was excruciating to watch. Julie was on her hands and knees within feet of the finish line when the second-place runner passed Julie to win the race. A few seconds later, Julie crawled across the finish line in one of the most dramatic finishes in sports history—and in the defining moment in Julie's life.

At some point every one of us will have a defining moment like the one Julie experienced in her Ironman. Julie's was captured on film and viewed by millions of people. She overcame intense physical demands and mental anguish in her efforts to achieve her goal. This moment in time redefined for Julie her physical and mental abilities.

Faith is the assurance of things hoped for,
the conviction of things not seen.
{ HEBREWS 11:1 NASB }

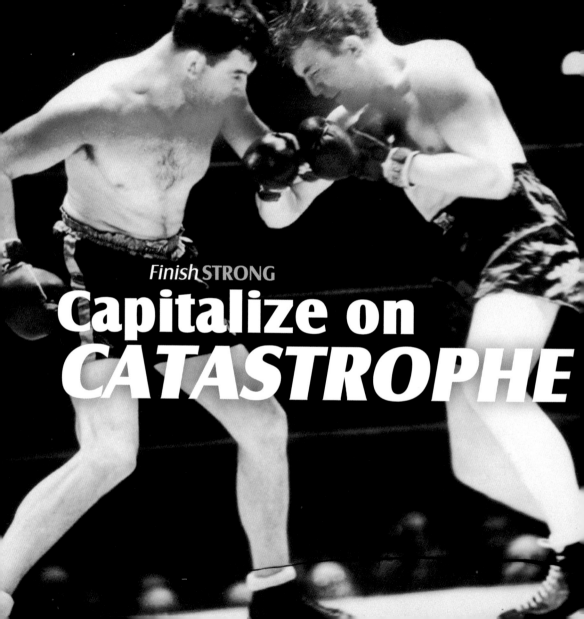

Finish STRONG
Capitalize on
CATASTROPHE

The finish strong story of Jim J. Braddock, the Cinderella Man, is one of my favorites. It's about a working man's rise to the top, his fall to the very bottom, and then his ascension to heights he never imagined. And as he traveled this journey, he discovered the true meaning of life.

Jim Braddock spent the better part of the 1920s boxing as a light heavyweight. During this time, he gained the reputation of being a fierce competitor who had a right-hand punch that could stop a bulldozer. His rise through the professional ranks began in 1926. He won most of his fights and earned a respectable reputation and living. By all accounts Jim Braddock was a successful man with a good life.

Braddock's first big chance came on a warm summer night in 1929 when he faced Tommy Loughran for the light heavyweight championship of the world. Loughran was a young and bright fighter who knew how dangerous Braddock's right hand could be. He studied Braddock's style and went into the fight with a strategy for avoiding the right hand. His research paid off, and Braddock was never able to land a solid punch with his right. The fight went fifteen rounds, and Braddock lost the decision to Loughran. And Braddock took this loss very hard.

With this loss, everything Braddock had worked to achieve seemed to be gone—and little did he know how much harder things would get. Less than two months after his loss to Loughran—on September 3, 1929—the stock market crashed and plunged America into the Great Depression.

6-22
AFTER LOUGHRAN LOSS

Like millions of Americans, Jim Braddock lost everything in the crash. With no work available, Jim continued to box in order to provide for his family. Unfortunately, his boxing career hit the skids during this time. He lost sixteen of twenty-two fights. To make matters worse, he shattered his powerful right hand and lost his greatest boxing asset. Under pressure to support his family, Braddock quit boxing and filed for government relief.

For the next few years, he struggled to make ends meet. He worked odd jobs on the docks and took whatever other work he could find.

His family finances grew worse; at times they had very little food or heat for their apartment. But during these tough years, Jim Braddock discovered not only how important his family was but also the true meaning of winning.

Have you noticed that God's timing is never early and never late? This was certainly true for Jim Braddock in 1934. Because of a last-minute cancellation and the dogged determination of his manager, he had the opportunity to fight on the undercard for the heavyweight championship bout between Max Baer and Primo Carnera at Madison Square Garden. There were, however, compelling reasons for him not to fight. For one, this was a heavyweight fight, and Braddock was not a heavyweight fighter. In fact, he was almost forty pounds lighter than the average heavyweight. Also, Braddock's right hand was not the same as it had been, and he was uncertain whether it would hold up under the stress of a boxing match. Finally, Braddock had not even been training for the fight. But none of this mattered to Jim.

What Braddock saw in this invitation to box was an opportunity to make some money and help his family. As slight as that chance was, he believed he could win, and that meant a better future for his family. Winning now meant so much more than it had before. With no training and a bum right hand, Braddock would shock the boxing community by knocking out John Griffin in the third round. He later said that his time spent working on the docks had kept him in shape and also helped him to develop a strong left hook—which no opponent expected.

As word of the upset spread, Braddock's popularity grew, and fight promoters would leverage this popularity to their advantage. As a result, he was given a shot at John Henry Lewis, a fighter who had previously beaten him. Although he was a huge underdog, Braddock delivered with a tenth-round victory. In doing so, Jim Braddock became an inspiration to a nation that desperately needed something to cheer about. Millions of working Americans appreciated him and his story.

In the spring of 1935, Braddock was matched up against Art Lasky, the number-one possible opponent to fight Max Baer, the reigning heavyweight champion. There was no discussion about Braddock getting a shot at Baer because nobody believed he could first beat Lasky. The fight promoters viewed this fight mostly as a way to capitalize on Braddock's popularity and to make a buck off of him. A Braddock victory did not even seem like an option. But he took Lasky to fifteen rounds, punishing Lasky so much that he won a unanimous decision.

With this victory, Braddock became the best candidate to fight Max Baer for the heavyweight championship of the world—still less than a year after working on the docks. The Cinderella Man had been born.

Jim Braddock faced Max Baer on June 13, 1935, at Madison Square Garden. Braddock entered the ring a 10–1 underdog and twenty pounds lighter than Baer, a ferocious fighter with a hammering right hand who had previously killed two other fighters in the ring. But Braddock had learned a valuable lesson from his earlier loss to Tommy Loughran: he had studied Baer's fight footage and identified a strategy for avoiding Baer's crushing right hand. Then, in one of the greatest upsets in all of sports history, the Cinderella Man battled Max Baer for fifteen rounds, won a unanimous decision, and was crowned heavyweight champion of the world.

In less than a year, Jim Braddock had turned his life completely around. Personal trials led him to both reevaluate his life and recognize an inner strength greater than he ever knew he had, and this new strength empowered his efforts to achieve his goals. When Braddock was given the opportunity to make a comeback, the mental shift he had made prepared him for the fight better than any physical training could have done. His new outlook on life impacted him long after his boxing career. He went on to lead a successful and prosperous life until his death in 1974.

15 ROUNDS
BRADDOCK VS. BAER

Finish STRONG

Discipline

Great beginnings are not as important
as the way one finishes.

DR. JAMES DOBSON

Nothing will work unless you do.

JOHN WOODEN

At the time, discipline isn't much fun.
It always feels like it's going against
the grain. Later, of course,
it pays off handsomely.

HEBREWS 12:11 MSG

Finish STRONG

Don't Let Life
PIN YOU
DOWN

Kyle Maynard loves to compete, and he knows that to truly live, you must set your sights on a goal and never give up until you reach it. This fire that burns in his belly led him all the way to the Georgia State High School wrestling championship in 2004. Not such a big deal, you might think—except for the remarkable fact that Kyle has no arms or legs. He was born a congenital amputee: his arms end at his elbows; his legs, at his knees.

The first time I saw Kyle was on an ESPN special in 2004 when he won an ESPY Award for Best Athlete with a Disability, and I was immediately struck by how normal he seemed. Kyle was doing all the things that any other person would do.

He spoke with passion and conviction, and he never gave the impression that he thought the world owed him anything. I was amazed to see him training hard, lifting weights (he has cannonballs for shoulders), and, using a specially designed attachment, pushing more than double his own body weight. I was instantly inspired to learn more about this amazing person.

From the beginning, Kyle's parents, Anita and Scott, were determined to raise a normal child. They insisted that Kyle learn to feed himself and play with the other kids like any child does.

> When Kyle saw other kids pick up crayons with their fingers, he learned to pick them up by using the crease in his short but sensitive biceps.

His grandmother Betty was a source of inspiration, and she often took Kyle to the grocery store, where she would instill in him a sense of confidence by encouraging him to sit up, look folks in the eye, and smile. Kyle was fitted with prosthetic devices at a young age, but he quickly dismissed them because they were too restrictive. He wanted to be free to run and play just like the other kids, and those devices kept him from doing so.

Kyle led an active childhood. He played street hockey with his friends (he was the goalie), and in sixth grade Kyle made the football team. He hung tough on the team, but his physical differences put him at a definite

KYLE MAYNARD

0-35

RECORD THROUGH HIS FIRST 35 MATCHES

disadvantage. Eventually, his father encouraged Kyle to try another sport, one that would put him on an even plane with his competition—wrestling.

Kyle started wrestling when he was in sixth grade—and he lost his first thirty-five matches. Needless to say, Kyle had to dig deep to find the confidence to continue. But he was a warrior, and he didn't like to lose. So with the support of his father, a former wrestler, Kyle learned to train with weights, became very strong, and learned some moves that played up his strengths. Kyle also overcame the self-doubt he had felt during his early wrestling days and became a winner. In his senior year, Kyle won thirty-five times on the varsity squad and qualified for the state championship. In the state tournament, Kyle won his first three matches and had to face his final opponent while he had a broken nose. Although Kyle did not win the championship, he had gained a high level of self-confidence and was a real inspiration for everyone he met.

There is no chance to fail if you never give up!
{ UNKNOWN }

After graduating from high school, Kyle went to the University of Georgia, where he continues to wrestle and inspire others. As a member of the Washington Speakers Bureau, Kyle is regularly asked to give motivational talks. But what he has to say has little to do with the physical challenges he faces. Instead, he talks about overcoming fear and doubt and what it takes to compete and win—topics any other champion would address.

To this day, Kyle has never been pinned by an opponent. What a fitting metaphor for his life.

35 WINS
IN HIS SENIOR YEAR

IT'S NOT WHAT WHAT HAPPENS TO YOU, BUT HOW YOU REACT TO IT THAT MATTERS.

EPICTETUS, AD 55-135

Finish **STRONG**

Believing Is
SEEING

Like the athletes featured in this book, Helen Keller also exemplified the finish strong spirit: she overcame great adversity and achieved success.

In 1880, Helen was born into an affluent Alabama family. At the age of nineteen months, Helen was stricken ill and left deaf and blind. Can you imagine the fear she must have felt when her world went dark and quiet? As the years progressed, Helen became wild and hard to control. If not for her young friend Martha Washington, the daughter of one of the family's servants, Helen might have been put into a sanitarium to live out her life. But Martha befriended Helen and taught her to communicate using sign language. Young Martha taught Helen over sixty different signs and truly helped Helen's world open up. Experts agree that Martha's assistance was critical to Helen's later success. When Helen was six, her mother was referred to a specialist who was working with deaf children: Alexander Graham Bell. After spending time with Helen, Mr. Bell referred her to the Perkins Institute for the Blind. That is where she met Annie Sullivan.

Annie was a twenty-year-old graduate of the school, and she was partially blind. (She had been completely blind but recovered part of her sight through a series of operations.) Annie understood Helen's dark world, so she asked permission to take Helen away from her family to help her focus. Once Helen was away, Annie was able to break her of her tantrums and ill behavior. Under Annie's guidance, Helen's world opened up exponentially.

> The marvelous richness of human experience would lose something of rewarding joy if there were no limitations to overcome. The hilltop hour would not be half so wonderful if there were no dark valleys to traverse.
>
> HELEN KELLER

Helen went on to become the first blind person ever to graduate from college. In addition to traveling the world as a famous speaker and author, Helen was an advocate for people with disabilities, amid numerous other causes. In 1915, she founded Helen Keller International, a nonprofit organization for preventing blindness. In 1920, she helped found the American Civil Liberties Union (ACLU). Helen and Annie became very close friends who traveled the world together meeting international dignitaries from more than forty countries. Helen also met every US president from Grover

Cleveland to Lyndon B. Johnson, and she was friends with many famous figures, including Alexander Graham Bell, Charlie Chaplin, and Mark Twain. Helen passed away in 1968 at the age of eighty-seven.

What enabled a deaf and blind six-year-old, born in the 1800s, to rise to such prominence and make such a difference in the world?

Without question, Martha Washington, Annie Sullivan, and Helen's mother have to be given a great deal of credit. But Helen's success also stemmed from her deep-seated desire to learn and to rise above the challenges before her. Without that drive, Helen could not have overcome her physical limitations, regardless of how much help she had. In her own way and outside the world of sports, Helen Keller was a champion who clearly finished strong.

Finish STRONG

Risk

Play the game for more
than you can afford to lose . . .
only then will you learn the game.

WINSTON CHURCHILL

People who take risks are the people
you'll lose against.

JOHN SCULLEY

Only those who will risk going too far can
possibly find out how far they can go.

T. S. ELIOT

Success is never final; failure is never
fatal. It's courage that counts.

JOHN WOODEN

Finish STRONG
Live with No
REGRETS

I was a freshman at Oklahoma State in 1983 when the Nebraska Cornhuskers came to town to play our Cowboys. The Cornhuskers had dominated all of their opponents and were the number-one team in college football when they came to Stillwater.

They had opened their season by crushing Penn State, the defending national champions, 44–6. Prior to coming to Stillwater, the Huskers had outscored their opponents 289–56.

I remember the game as if it were yesterday because, although we lost 14–10, we gave Nebraska their first and only real scare that year. It was a heartbreaking loss for us. However, it was also very memorable because of the great players I got to see. Mike Rozier would go on to win the Heisman Trophy that year, Turner Gill was an absolute wizard at quarterback, and wide receiver Irving Fryar would ultimately become the number-one draft pick in the NFL.

In 1983, the head coach for Nebraska was Tom Osborne. He had never won a national championship and was under tremendous pressure to do so, and by all accounts he was on his way to bringing Nebraska their first championship. His offense was probably the greatest college offense ever to take the field. They finished their season with a perfect record and entered the Orange Bowl as the number-one team in the country. There they would face the Miami Hurricanes. The Hurricanes had entered the season unranked and were slaughtered in their opener by seventh-ranked Florida. That, however, would be their first and only loss of the season. After that game, the Hurricanes dominated every game they played. As a result, they entered the Orange Bowl ranked fourth in the nation.

Two key games had been decided prior to the Orange Bowl. The number-two Texas Longhorns were upset in the Cotton Bowl by number-three Georgia, and the Auburn Tigers put away Michigan in the Sugar Bowl. As a result, the Orange Bowl would be played for the national title.

Of course, the game was hyped by the media as the game of the century. Could the previously unknown Hurricanes actually win? Would Tom Osborne get his first national title? Could the Nebraska offense actually be stopped? The game lived up to the hype. An emotional rollercoaster, the game came down to the last two minutes. With 1:46 left to play, the Cornhuskers had the ball on Miami's twenty-six-yard line on fourth down with eight yards to go. They were trailing Miami 31–24. In one of the greatest

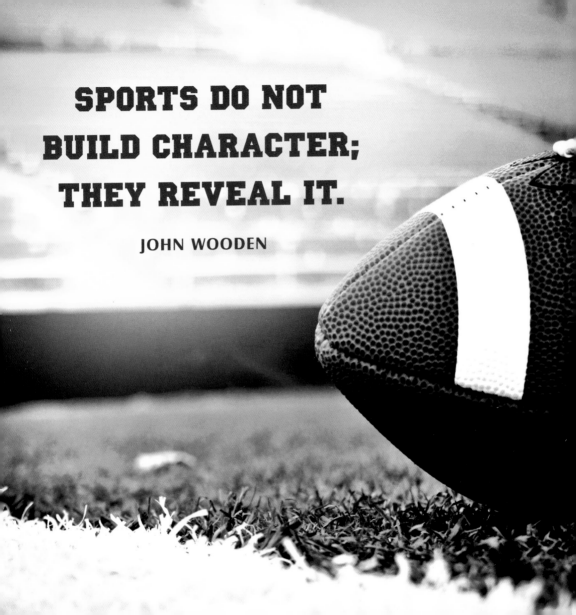

SPORTS DO NOT BUILD CHARACTER; THEY REVEAL IT.

JOHN WOODEN

NOBODY who ever gave his best regretted it.

GEORGE HALAS

plays in college football history, Turner Gill ran the option to the right and pitched the ball to Jeff Smith, who ran it in for a touchdown and pulled the Cornhuskers within one point with under a minute left to play. They could tie the game with an extra point, or they could win outright with a two-point conversion. There was no overtime to decide an outright winner. A tie game would leave the championship to be decided by the coaches and media polls, but an outright win would seal the championship for the Huskers.

The decision was Coach Osborne's. He put the championship on the line and went for two points and the win. He had the best run offense in the country and was completely confident that the team could pull it off. He also knew that Miami would be expecting the run. So instead of using his bread-and-butter run offense, he opted to pass the ball. Gill's pass fell incomplete, and after a failed onside kick, Nebraska lost its first game of the year—and the national championship.

The next morning, football fans across the country debated the "go-for-two" call. Many argued that, given a tie, Nebraska would have easily won the vote for the title. Osborne and his team had a different perspective. They wanted to finish strong. They wanted to win the game and the championship outright, and they took the path they believed would get them there. It was a calculated risk that, in this instance, didn't work, but the Cornhuskers gave it their best shot. To this day, Coach Osborne does not regret it.

Finish STRONG

BEGINNINGS

We've gotten to the final chapter, and I'm sure you've recognized the theme throughout. For most of these champions, their great accomplishment was not the end of their greatness; rather it was the beginning of greater things to come. Each person profiled here used the moment in time you read about to propel him- or herself forward in life.

After the shark attack, Bethany Hamilton became a world-class surfer and an inspiration to thousands of people around the world. After he achieved his success in boxing, Jim Braddock repaid the government the aid money he had received during his hard times and went on to live a full and prosperous life. John Baker's commitment to give his best effort lives on at the elementary school bearing his name. After her Olympic glory, Wilma Rudolph championed civil rights causes and, as a teacher, inspired thousands of children.

The finish strong attitude is grounded in the principle that none of us ever "arrives" in life, so we should always keep moving forward. I love what Olympic swimming champion John Naber said. When asked if winning four Olympic gold medals was the highlight of his life, he replied, "I hope not! I've still got a lot of living left to do, and I hope my greatest achievement is still in front of me."

May your greatest achievements still be in front of you—and may you always *Finish* **STRONG.**

EFFORT ONLY FULLY RELEASES ITS REWARD AFTER A PERSON REFUSES TO QUIT.

NAPOLEON HILL

I have fought the good fight,
I have finished the race,
I have kept the faith.

2 TIMOTHY 4:7

ABOUT THE AUTHOR

Dan is an entrepreneur with a passion for finishing strong in everything he does. Over the past twenty years, he has excelled in his roles as salesman, sales leader, sales trainer, patented inventor, race car driver, author, and speaker. The finish strong attitude has been a driving force in Dan's life and a key catalyst in his achieving his goals in business, sports, and life. He currently serves as a partner and executive vice president with Simple Truths and is the founder of Finish Strong, LLC.

Dan is the author of three inspirational books—*Finish Strong, Finish Strong Teen Athlete*, and *Finish Strong Motivational Quotes*—and has sold more than 250,000 copies worldwide. The first *Finish Strong* book provided Drew Brees and the New Orleans Saints a guiding theme on their way to a Super Bowl victory.

Since 1996, when he received the trademark rights to the words *Finish Strong*, Dan has been an evangelist for this message of challenge and inspiration. Thousands of people from all walks of life have adopted the finish strong attitude and applied it in their lives, to overcome adversity and to achieve their dreams.

Dan lives outside Chicago with his wife and two daughters.

For more information about Dan, to inquire
about speaking engagements, or to learn more about
incorporating Finish Strong into your next event,
e-mail **contact@finishstrong.com**
or visit **www.finishstrong.com**.

Finish
STRONG